THE WOUND

Versions of C.P. Cavafy

David Harsent

DARE-GALE PRESS

First published in Great Britain by Dare-Gale Press, 2025

www.daregale.com

ISBN 9781915968111

Front cover image created by Athens Surreal, reproduced by kind permission of the Onassis Foundation.

Font: Typeset in 10/11pt Delicato, designed by Stefan Hattenbach.

Printed in England by One Digital Brighton on GF Smith paper certified by both Cradle to Cradle and the Forest Stewardship Council. Dare-Gale Press is committed to environmentally conscious publishing. For our environmental policy please visit www.daregale.com.

In selecting poems by Cavafy to render into English versions, I have chosen, most often, poems of love and loss. Among these are poems whose subject, in part, is age, though love and loss are ever present: evidence of waste, of missed chances, of betrayal. Fractured memory recalls brief, passionate, affairs ending in sudden, almost expected, desertion and emotional torment. Love as broken glass.

In the poem that ends this small collection, 'What's Hidden', Cavafy says, *One day / when times and laws and minds have changed / someone who thinks and feels and loves like me / will live as I do now, but without fear.* That speaks to the weight of sorrow in these poems, but also to their (the poet's) resilience, to their lyric insistence, and to an unashamed delight in the pleasures of the flesh.

D.H.
June, 2025

At the Tobacconist's Window

A small crowd at the brightly-lit window
and these two, these among many...
Their eyes, as if meant to, snag softly,
then they walk off, although maybe
unsure until one smiles discreetly
and catches a nod — only barely.
They drive, they park up. They are so
careful about how best to go
here and go there, lips and hands going slow
as they fall on each other, but gently.

The Art of Poetry

They get out of bed. They get dressed,
a touch shaky, now, as they leave,
one going this way, one that,
and it's easy enough to guess
from each wide-eyed look as they pass
that enough was too much to give.

Nothing unusual in this,
but the poet has just found a rhyme
for a song that will start with the line
They get out of bed. They get dressed...

Afternoon Sun

The room is up for rent, a room
I know so well. They are renting out
every room in the house, a house of rooms
now rented to agents, to clerks, to businessmen.

A sofa stood by the door, a Turkish rug
in front of the sofa; on that shelf
two yellow vases and off to the right,
no, opposite, a wardrobe, its full-length mirror,
then a table, a pen, a poem half-done,
three wicker armchairs — yes,
and beside the window, our bed...

(Perhaps that old stuff has fetched up
somewhere in other rooms, in other lives.)

...beside the window, our bed.
The afternoon sun
crept over it as we lay there: over us.

At four o'clock on one such afternoon
we parted
for just a week...a week or so...forever.

That Night

The room was squalid and the bar below
dog-rough: on a trash-strewn alley
where navvies dealt cards and yelled the odds.

Many had come before to the narrow bed
where I had that perfect body, had my fill
of those wine-red lips, so skilled
in love's ways that now, years later,
alone in this lonely house, I'm drunk again.

Windows

Dark house, dark days... I go from room to room
in search of windows: an open window

would make all the difference; but this
is a blind house: there are no windows, or else

I can't find them. But what if I did —
what if I found a window and opened it?

What if I let in a tyranny of light?

The Souls of Old Men

The souls of old men lie skin-deep
in their wasted bodies. Old men,

they have worn out and it shows,
they are tired of life and it shows.

Even so, they fear death. Old men
holding on to life though it bores them,

loving life though it grieves them.
Tragicomic, just skin-deep, and it shows.

The Mirror in the Hallway

A beautiful boy came to the house with a package.
A tailor's assistant; on Sundays
he played park football. A factotum
took the package and left to get a receipt.

There's a mirror in the entrance hall;
it was hung when the house was first built
eighty years ago. The boy
went to the mirror and looked at himself.
He straightened his tie. He looked at himself.

The mirror looked back. In eighty years
it had seen a thousand faces and shrugged them off.
It held that matchless beauty
long minutes after the boy had gone.

Voices

Voices we loved, voices of the dead, of those
who are gone from us and might as well be dead,
speak to us in dreams
or when we are lost in thought, they find us.

Half-forgotten voices bring in
half-forgotten music from our first poems,
night-music, distant, fading...

Her Prayer

A woman lights a candle before an ikon of Our Lady
and prays for the safe return of her son, a sailor;
she prays for good weather; she listens to the wind.

This morning, a sailor was taken by the sea.
The Holy Virgin attends in sadness,
knowing the woman's son is lost to her.

Come Evening

Well, it wouldn't have lasted, experience told me that,
but cold Fate took a hand, so it was sudden:
our time together gone, the end of things.

Yet how could I forget those perfumes,
that sumptuous bed where we gave
such pleasure each to each?

Those days came back to me, the fierce
heat of youth. I found that final letter
and read it again and again in the fading light.

Now I've come onto the balcony. Perhaps
a sight of the city I love might shift my sadness:
the cafes, the shops, people in the street...

An Old Man

Alone at the back of the café,
in a hubbub of voices, an old man sits
bent over the table, his evening paper unread.

Old age weighs on him.
He thinks of the wasted years
when he had good health, good looks.

He's old, he knows it, feels it, sees it:
face, hands, body; days of pain;
but his youth seems only yesterday.

He remembers Caution, the bitch deceiver —
that he believed her when she said,
'Take it easy: there's time for everything.'

So he held back on lust, on love, on joy;
now all he knows is loss and loss
laughs at him from the prison of missed chances.

He thinks on this until misery makes him ill.
He puts his old grey head
on the café table and waits for sleep.

Monotony

One dreary day, another dreary day.
What happened yesterday will happen again today,
this moment will come and go and come and go.

One dreary month, another dreary month.
You can guess the rest: what happened
will happen again, that tireless boredom
when today is tomorrow and tomorrow is today.

I Went

I let go. I couldn't hold back.
I went to those lovely sins:
some sought and found, some fierce imaginings...

The night was ablaze. I went there
and drank the heavy wine
that only the bravest of sinners dares to drink.

Advice to a Poet

Your daydreams of love and lust:
treasure them, slip them into your lines
(a hint, no more) but keep them close,
whether they come at night or in the midday glare.

Come Back

Come back, possess me, come back
again and again, sensation, emotion,
ghost-love, come back,
take hold of me when my body summons
an old passion that fires my blood,
when eager hands and lips touch skin again.

Come back, take hold of me, possess me.
Come at night
when lips and hands go there again.

Grey Opals

This opal's pale grey lustre reminds me of his eyes;
it was twenty years ago, or maybe more...

We were lovers. After a month, he left: a job
in Smyrna, I think. Yes...yes, it was Smyrna.
And that was the end of it. I never saw him again.

Those opal eyes will have faded now, of course;
his beauty, too. In memory, I hold him as he was.

And, memory, all I ask
is bring it back unchanged, that brief lost love.

Bring it back tonight...

The Sea at Morning

I'll stop a while and look at the view
as anyone might: bright blue of the morning sea,
a cloudless sky, the foreshore swamped with light.

I'll stop and pretend that's all I see,
(which, for a moment, it was) when, in truth,
those fantasies of flesh-on-flesh crowd in.

The Wound

He said he'd fallen; there was more to it than that...
He reached up to the shelf for a photo-album.
The wound opened; blood ran down his arm.

I changed the bandage. He wasn't in pain,
so I took my time. I wanted to see the blood.
That blood had mingled with my love.

After he'd gone, I found the stained
bandage I'd dropped on the floor.
Blood of love. I held it to my lips.

The City

Another country, another sea, another city --
it's time! Everything I do here turns to dust.
My heart lies dead within me; how long
can my mind endure this slow decay?
Wherever I look I see the wreckage of my days.
I have wasted my life in this place.

That will never happen. Another city? No. You'll walk
these same streets, grow old in one of the houses
in this same neighbourhood. Don't hope
for the fabled 'elsewhere': whatever ship you take,
whatever road, this city will go with you,
just as your ruined life goes with you everywhere.

The Chandelier

An empty room, four walls draped in green.
A chandelier, its candles burning.
This is no simple light.
Each flame ignites a fever of desire,
too hot for the fainthearted.

Pleasures of the Flesh

The best of it: that I chose both love and lover
and had them on my terms. That I never fell
into a sad routine of one-night stands.

Despair

His lover is lost to him: completely lost. Now he finds
his lover in every boy he takes to bed. Behind closed eyes
the body he holds is still his lover's body.

His lover is lost to him: yes, lost and gone. 'I can't
live like this,' he'd said, 'this shame, this sordid life.
I'll find another way. Think of me as dead.'

His lover is lost to him: no help for that, no hope.
But the boys he takes to bed become his lover: he knows it
by the way their love-tricks play out on his skin.

Days of 1903

I looked, but never found those haunted eyes,
pale features, lost to the night-time streets.

I never found again those things I got by chance,
so easily given up, so badly missed.

I looked but never found them, haunted eyes...
Oh, and lips, those red lips got by chance.

At the Casino

How old do you think he is? Twenty? Twenty-two?
Well, it was twenty years ago (say twenty-two)
when I had that body, that boy, I'm sure of it.

No, I'm not drunk: I only just arrived.
That boy, that body, yes...
Don't ask me where, it was twenty years ago.

He's come to the table next to us. Now, look:
his gestures, his smile, oh, I remember –
his nakedness, the body I loved, that boy.

His Chosen Life

He went back to the bar where they first met.
He asked around. 'Who knows?' the waiters said,
'Could be your friend hooked up
with one of the shady types we see in here.'

*

He goes there every night to watch the door.
One week, two weeks, three, it wears him out.
He's half-mad with desire; his mouth is wet
as from his lover's kiss; his body trembles
as from his lover's touch.

*

Hot with desire, with hope, but he wears a public face,
faking indifference; and, for the merest moment,
indifference is what he feels; then that deep need floods back
and he's lost to a secret life that could spell his ruin.

In the Past

Blue eyes, I think...yes...I think they were blue...
so long ago...it comes back in dim-lit fragments.
I was young, in my teens, just a boy.

Skin scented with jasmine, I remember that.
It was August, or so I think; a night in August.
Jasmine skin...blue eyes...yes, sapphire blue...

His Vow

He vows to change his life, but then comes nightfall:
its own dark thoughts, excuses, sweet temptations.

Nightfall brings on the body's craving; he's drawn
helpless, again, to that dark forbidden pleasure.

House of Shame

As I was leaving, you came in the door.
We passed on the stairs.
We glanced at one another. I turned away.
You hid your face and hurried by.

I knew you would find no pleasure in that house:
I found none; yet what you wanted I had to give
and what I lacked I could have got from you;
our bodies knew: compulsion of flesh and blood.

You hid your face. I turned away.

Walls

Somehow, they built this prison round me,
bricks and mortar, sky-high.

Walled in, I think only of walls; it gnaws at me;
I have a life to live in the world outside.

How did they do this without my noticing?
Why didn't I see them: see them or hear them?

Such subtle skills. Now I'm dead to the world.

His Poems, His Dreams

An old man, bent-backed, worn to a nub
by the years, by the weight of shame,
shuffles across the narrow backstreet
and opens his door.
                                        Once inside, his age
and ugliness hidden, he thinks of how
he keeps pace with the young:
they read his poems, they recite his dreams.
His lines bring light to their eyes, his love of beauty
stirs their minds. It stirs their beautiful bodies.

What’s Hidden

Don’t look for me in what I said or did:
there was a hidden truth
that gave the lie to everything. I know
that only in my secret life, the dark
depth of my lines, could I be understood.

Don’t look; why take the trouble? One day,
when times and laws and minds have changed,
someone who thinks and feels and loves like me
will live as I do now, but without fear.